ARE COVID-19 PASSPORTS THE MARK OF THE BEAST

ARE COVID-19 PASSPORTS THE MARK OF THE BEAST

JAMES WHITELAW

Swackie Ltd

CONTENTS

Are Covid-19 Passports the Mark of the Beast

by

James G Whitelaw

[16] And he causeth all, both small and great, rich and poor, free and bond, to receive a mark in their right hand, or in their foreheads:

[17] And that no man might buy or sell, save he that had the mark, or the name of the beast, or the number of his name.

[18] Here is wisdom. Let him that hath understanding count the number of the beast: for it is the number of a man; and his number is Six hundred threescore and six.**Introduction**

Introduction

Many governments are starting to talk about the introduction of Covid-19 passports. Some society members are very concerned about this, seeing the possibility of abuse of the data collected. Critics pointed to how Youtube, Facebook, and Twitter have de-platformed users who do not comply with their mindest. These mega tech companies have destroyed some businesses that they deem inappropriate. This has been very much pronounced in right-leaning news stations that have not agreed with the mainstream media.

In this book, we examine what Covid-19 passports could mean for you and ask the simple question, "Are Covid-19 passports the mark of the beast?".

We will look at what the 'Mark of the beast' is, what it would look like, how it might operate, what benefits it has, what drawbacks it has, and the consequences of not going along with this scheme.

It is not a very comfortable subject to read about, but necessary to know what is coming down the line at some point in the future. It may not be Covid-19 passports, and perhaps I am over pessimistic, but even if it does not happen this time, it will happen at some point and better to be prepared.

If governments press ahead with Covid-19 passports and those who do not have them become second rate citizens, how would it affect you? What would it mean to you? Read on to find out.

Jim Whitelaw is a committed Christian who is familiar with what is predicted in the end times. He sees what is coming down the line and how it ties in with the word of God. This is a subject that is very much in the news and very controversial. You must read what he says.

Contents

CHAPTER 1

What is the mark of the beast?

Christians have long known about the 'Mark of the beast'. The scriptures we read on the first page were given to them around 1,900 years ago. It wasn't easy to understand precisely how this could work in practice until relatively recently, but it is now considered not only possible but very simple with modern technology.

The disciple, John, who is believed to have been the last of the disciples of Jesus to die, was a very old man. Christianity was even more offensive to the ruling classes than it is today. The rulers saw Christianity as a threat to their absolute control. This is little different from what we see in communist China, North Korea and most Islamic countries.

If Christianity was a threat, it had to be stamped out, eradicated, obliterated and wholly erased from the people's memories. Thus, many disciples and followers were imprisoned and killed, most in horrible, excruciating deaths, so great were the rulers' hatred against peace-loving Christians.

John, the disciple, was banished to a small island called Patmos, which is off the coast of modern-day Turkey. While John was on Patmos, he was given a revelation of things to come, which we now know as the 'Book of revelation', the last book of the Bible. There are many pointers to how the world will develop within this revelation, but the verses we are concerned with now are in chapter 13, verses 16 through 18.

Let us take a look at this 'mark of the beast' and examine what it is and what it means to us today. Finally, let us ask the main question, 'are Covid-19 passports the mark of the beast?'

It is unclear precisely what form the mark will take, but it will be an identification mark that encompasses the entire world, having authority in every place. Those who do not have the mark will not be able to buy and sell, making it almost impossible to live, eat and drink. The Bible calls this period the 'Great Tribulation' and says that there has never been such a difficult time in history. Those who choose not to accept the mark of the beast are specially destined for a difficult time.

Many have speculated about what form the mark will take, and theories abound around plastic cards, citizen ID cards, the world wide web and such, but none have come to fruition. I wish, in this book, to put forward another theory, which may or may not come to fruition, yet I feel it is one of the most credible threats to date. It makes me feel very uncomfortable.

For the mark to be successful, as seen from through the eyes of the 'beast', it must be able to control every aspect of the lives of those who carry it and record all the data about them. It must also become mandatory to have it, with severe penalties for those who do not comply. To achieve this, a significant number, but not necessarily the majority, must be convinced of its necessity.

Could Covid-19 passports pass these tests? It is certainly plausible and examining how the public has readily accepted the restrictions imposed on them over the past year, and it would seem reasonably likely that they would accept a further measure 'in the country's interests and to protect the general population'.

It is not only governments calling for the introduction of Covid-19 passports, but also big businesses like airlines, hotels, etc. Governments prefer if others call for action, and they are seen only to be supplying the answer. In many cases, government plants a seed in other ears, lets them do the pushing, and make it seem like they are reluctantly providing the answer. There is no end to the smoke and mirrors in politics. Anything a politician says should never be taken at face value, especially if they are in a position of power.

Of course, we do have to consider whether our leading politicians are, in fact, in power or if they are merely puppets for a paymaster, but that is a whole different debate.

If Covid-19 passports are the mark of the beast, you can be sure this did not originate in a government department but rather somewhere like Davos. Looking at how the talk of Covid-19 passports is coming out, it seems that the roll-out is co-ordinated and, therefore, some higher authority has carefully planned and is pushing this agenda.

Those pushing for a world-wide government received a massive setback in 2016, firstly with the Brexit result and secondly by Donald Trump's election. I believe they have doubled down on efforts to make sure this never happens again and redoubled efforts to ensure they tighten control of every major country in the world.

CHAPTER 2

How would the mark of the beast be beneficial?

What would be the purpose of a Covid-19 vaccine, and what would entice the general population to go along with the plan?

We have been bombarded with statistics over the past year about how many people are dying from Covid-19. Millions of people have died from this deadly pandemic, and we were warned that failure to comply with the restrictions put in place would result in enormous amounts of casualties.

Something didn't seem right to me, so I decided to look at the raw statistics for myself and try and determine whether it was as bad as they were making out. I went to the national register for Scotland and downloaded the official figures for total deaths over the last few years, and I was shocked by what I found.

In Moray, my home territory, total deaths for 2020 were lower than the previous two years and lower than the five-year average. For the entire nation of Scotland, total deaths were 11.7 per thousand of the population in 2020, as opposed to an average of 10.95 over the preceding 25 years. It was a high year, but four out of the previous 25 years were higher, so it is not unprecedented.

I used the total deaths figures, as these, in my view, were the only figures which the government could not manipulate. They publish figures of so many deaths 'with Covid-19', but these include people who were on the point of death, then caught the virus in hospital. They also include people who died of a longstanding illness but also had Covid. The figures are manipulated and presented to scare the general population into submission to draconian measures.

Never before, in the world's history, have we shut down the economy. We have gone through terrible wars, famines, pestilences and even the bubonic plague, in which one-third of Europe died, but never has anyone ever contemplated shutting down the economy of the world. In 2020 though, our enlightened leaders thought it was different this time.

One could be forgiven for thinking that it all had a feeling of co-ordination, and now, once again, right on cue, all the world's leaders are starting to talk about Covid-19 passports. What would the benefits of these passports be? What are they telling us is the compelling requirement for these documents?

It's all in the name of protecting everyone from infection and possible death. It is about ensuring the disease does not spread. It is about reducing the numbers infected to as low as possible. Going out for a meal or a drink would be very dangerous, so if only vaccinated people were allowed to enter these establishments, we could deny the virus the opportunity to spread.

Boarding a flight, a train or even a bus carries a grave risk to all passengers, so it is reasonable only to allow vaccinated passengers to board, to reduce that risk, likewise with hotels, offices, shops, factories and all manner of places. All are at risk, but if we can restrict entrance to people who have been vaccinated, then we can control that risk.

Let us examine what the scientists have told us about the vaccine. It does not stop you from catching the virus. It does not prevent you from spreading the virus. It does not eradicate the virus. So anyone who has had the vaccine can still have the virus, can still spread the virus, can still even die from the virus, so why would a vaccine passport be any benefit?

It seems that this is simply a fantastic opportunity for them to roll out a system for which they have longed to have. It is a system that would give them complete control over the entire population, without exception—the power of life and death overall.

This is very concerning, so we will examine the Vaccine passports' downsides and the risks for you if you accept them in the next chapter.

CHAPTER 3

What are the drawbacks of having the mark?

The US government are currently considering the roll-out of vaccine passports. Andy Slavitt, the acting director for the Centers for Medicare and Medicaid Services, recently said, "the government here is not viewing its role as the place to create a passport, nor a place to hold the data of citizens. We view that as something that the private sector is doing and will do".

Do you find it rather strange that all the world governments are starting to talk about vaccine passports, almost in unison? Consider the statement above. The US government would not build a system themselves but would enable or approve a third-party contractor to complete the project.

Would this be similar to Twitter or Facebook running the world's media system? Think about the power that these companies have. They recently de-platformed a sitting US president because they didn't like what he said. What could they do if they had the power to prevent you from entering restaurants, offices, factories or even shops? How would you move around if you were denied access and boarding rights to planes, trains and buses?

Are you beginning to see the power these companies could command over you? Can you imagine the situation where three couples booked into a restaurant for a meal, scanned their passports and were admitted? The database holder knows where you are, knows who you are with, knows even what you are eating, and eavesdropping through your mobile phones, even know what you are all talking about during your meal.

They could quickly draw up a complete picture of all your movements, friends and acquaintances, and even the way you think. Take the example a little further. It has been flagged that someone in your group said something inappropriate. Your passports are automatically downgraded, and the next day when you want to go to the cinema, you are denied access.

When you go home, you notice an email with details of a possible breach of the conditions for the use of your passport. You are warned that this withdrawal of rights is a warning that you must moderate your future behaviour. There are veiled warnings that continuing to breach your agreement may result in further restrictions.

One of your friends is especially annoyed about this and takes to social media to spout off about its injustice and how it is an infringement of his rights. The next day, going shopping, he is denied entry to the supermarket. He is flagged as a danger to society and can not access any common space for five days, and is warned that further breaches may result in a permanent ban.

Your entire group receive an email saying that one of your friends has been identified as a danger to society. If you continue to consort with this individual, you risk a permanent downgrade to your status.

Is this a real danger, a real possibility? Judge for yourself by how these big corporations have treated some society members. If they can de-platform a sitting president of the most powerful nation on earth, then they can, and will, de-platform anyone.

This example is not far fetched. It is simply how these media giants are operating now. Their actions in de-platforming some people have had profound impacts on their lives, but at least they cannot ban users from going to the supermarket, which they could do with a Covid-19 passport.

If any person, organisation or government were to obtain this level of power, it would only be a matter of time before it was abused and some lives ruined for thinking the wrong way.

CHAPTER 4

Could the mark control all our lives?

We find it incredible that one corporation could attain such control over our lives. Is it possible? Likely? Would not our governments step in to prevent the abuse of power and stop them from achieving such dictatorial status?

I can only look to what has been happening over the past few years to the right-leaning media companies and have to conclude, yes, it is possible, and it certainly is likely. The extraordinary lengths some of these companies, or government exercising control through these companies, have gone to silence some right-leaning journalists would have been unbelievable only ten years ago in the UK and reminded you more of Soviet Russia or communist China.

Do a search on Youtube for 'Alex Belfield, The Voice of reason', see how the BBC has controlled and used the police to harass and intimidate him. Research the extraordinary lengths they have gone to in an attempt to ruin his life utterly. What was his crime? He was a whistleblower at the BBC after serving them for 15 years as a journalist.

Do another deep search for 'Tommy Robinson'. Tommy tried to highlight the scale of the rape problem of English girls by Pakistani Muslims in England. The government did not want this to be common knowledge, so they silenced Tommy after a very long intimidation campaign, which resulted in him being jailed twice, hauled through courts, and sentenced in a kangaroo court, which was later overturned.

Tommy was particularly uncompliant and refused to back down, so the government agencies upped their game and started targeting Tommy's family until they eventually silenced him. Now, we no longer hear anything from Tommy. It is quite simply not worth the destruction of his family to fight against the system. The power that these companies already have is astonishing, but these are the companies who are vying to run your new Covid-19 passport system.

If you research how they silenced Tommy, you will quickly understand that if we let them get this level of control over us, we will be left with no option but to become 'model citizens'. Any opposition, however small, will be severely dealt with, and no dissent will be tolerated.

There are many more examples of complete despotic control within our democracy, all dressed up for the majority's good. If you then research into the beginnings of Stalin's Russia, Hitler's Germany, or any other dictatorship, you will find the same trends that we see now in the western world. My concern now is of a greater magnitude, though, as this time, the elites are attempting this on a global scale, and there will be no untouched country to come to our rescue.

The UK, The USA, Canada, New Zealand, Australia, all bastions of democracy, so it is hard to believe that this could happen in our countries. I'm sure that Germany thought that before the rise of Adolf Hitler, and even now, looking back, many Germans find it incomprehensible that the country could have gone along with his plans.

All dictators sound very plausible at the outset. They must give this image to assert control, but once complete control is gained, the benevolence is dropped, and the monster appears. This can happen anywhere, and monsters are all around us. The USA's founding fathers understood this and tried to write checks and balances into the USA's constitution. President Biden is now trying to set aside these rights the people have, claiming the good of the entire nation. Nothing must allow our rights to be set aside ever. That is the only way we can retain protection. Once it is gone, we are slaves of those that control us.

It is a little more difficult in the UK, as we have no written constitution. However, we have our bill of rights, dating back to 1688 and the Magna Carta dating from 1215. These are potent documents that have underpinned our democracy for eight hundred years and must not be allowed to be set aside now. If we allow these documents to be overruled, we will be slaves to the rulers, whoever they may be. For this precise reason, the Magna Carta was signed in 1215 to stop King John from abusing his power.

The only protection the ordinary man in the street has is dictated in these two documents where we are always guaranteed to be free. More than that, we are obliged to take up arms against anyone who attempts to take away that freedom from us.

There is a particular danger in the EU, which is a society ruled by unelected bureaucrats, and it may be the saving of the UK that we are no longer any part of this evil empire.

Governments now seek to pass that power to third parties under the guise of protecting the whole. However, the result will be to give this unlimited power to an organisation which we have no control of, can not vote for or vote out, should they decide to carry out measures not approved by us, the people.

Of late, governments are even denying the right to protest, again under the guise that it is for the whole country's good. Under our bill of rights and the Magna Carta, we have the privilege of protest, which cannot be removed under any circumstances. This right must be protected and vigorously defended.

In recent years, it has been a particular trait of all governments to create an independent body to oversee areas where the public is concerned and don't trust the government. In the UK, we call them government quangos. The government then appoint the 'independent chief of the quango' who will naturally pay heed to those who pay his wages and keep him in a job.

The second stage of a quango is to secure it in a position recognised as the independent authority. After this, every time the government want to back up their plans, this independent authority confirms all is good. It is all smoke and mirrors.

Overall, our political systems in the western world are rotten to the core, with no exception, which I have discovered. We may well find that if we get into a mess, it will be a country like Russia that eventually helps us.

CHAPTER 5

What will happen if we refuse the mark?

The Bible tells us if we do not have the mark, we will not be able to buy or sell, and we now see this put forward as an aim of our government. It has been suggested that we will need a passport before we can go for a pint and before we can use public transport, to name but a few examples.

Usually, if government produces a law, it is then added to and constantly expanded to cover much more than initially envisaged. One law is often used as a back door into another area, where our rights to freedom are further eroded without our consent. Due to this subtleness, the vast majority of the people no longer trust politicians. The population continually see the erosion of their freedoms, the increasingly heavy burden of taxation, and their rights to free speech being curtailed daily.

We have always had a policy in the UK of policing by consent. Even the most compliant of us all recognise that we are well beyond this point now, with increased police brutality being reported everywhere this past year. If we give the government or another organisation the power to control us, consent will not be required, and we will be like sheep herded in flocks to be model citizens.

Even to a benevolent leader or group, this power level must never be given. Once it is given, it can never be taken back, and it is only a matter of time before someone abuses this power. We have all seen multiple cases of abuse of power recently and noticed this tendency to increase with the level of government corruption.

We quite rightly do not trust politicians and therefore must conclude that we can neither trust them with this power level over us or by an 'independent quango' holding this power. We have seen the draconian measures introduced over the past year without these powers. Imagine how it would be policed if they have unlimited powers over your life.

This idea of Covid-19 passports must be stopped in its tracks. If a substantial amount of the population goes along with this, we are doomed. If required, we must take massive action to stop this from coming into being in either a mandated or voluntary way. Even if it starts voluntary, that will only be a step towards a mandated version. We must educate the population about the powers that the rulers have planned for them and how they wish to control them.

It will certainly not be an easy fight. These people have money, loads of it and they will not rest easy and give up. We have seen how they tried to subvert the Brexit vote in the UK and how they undermined the power of the President of the strongest country in the world. Please make no mistake about it. They will not take it lying down. I fully expect them to come for me for even writing this book. Please ensure you have a hard copy of this book stored and downloaded somewhere, as I am pretty sure it will disappear from the shelves at some point.

We need to ready ourselves for a fight. If it is not this year, it will be a little further down the line. The elites got a real shock in 2016, and they are determined that there will never be another setback like that. It has made them all very more determined to complete this transformation as soon as possible.

If you think this all far fetched, then go to weforum.org/great-reset and see for yourself what they have planned, and remember, this is no government. This is a consortium of mega-companies.

CHAPTER 6

How will we recognise the mark?

That is a difficult question. The mark could take many forms. The only way to recognise it is its actions and potential. Remember what I said about it away back at the start of this book. It must be able to control every aspect of the lives of those who carry it. It must also become mandatory to have it, with severe penalties for those who do not comply.

The Bible talks about a mark in your forehead or your hand, which has led many to believe it will be an implanted chip, but this may not be its original form, and this may only be mandated after sufficient take-up.

The main thing to look out for is the consequences of non-participation. These may be pretty simple or mild initially but will set the trend to be escalated once complete control is achieved.

Many laws being introduced through parliament have been relatively vague in some areas in recent years. For example, the latest hate crime bill passed through the Scottish Parliament defined a hate crime as something a judge deems hateful to any reasonable person. That is pretty vague and very much dependent on the judge who listens to your case.

It is our feeling that the mark, when it appears, will make a lot of sense, but at the same time, there will be a difficulty by not accepting it. If you see something like this appear, then it is time to sit back and watch what happens. If it becomes apparent that it is gaining traction and there will be consequences of not going along with it, then the alarm bells should start ringing.

At this point, it is not going to be enough to sit back and decide to leave others to join up, and assure yourself you will ride it out. That is not going to happen. The more people who sign up to it, the more a hold it gets. The more hold it gets, the more you are left exposed. These people have no scruples, no morals; if half the population sign up, they will be only too happy to kill off the other half and be left with the compliant majority.

Genocide has happened in the past in many countries, even in Europe, during the last thirty years, in the Balkans. It most definitely can happen again. If you see this coming to pass, you must resist it with everything you have. Your life will depend on it.

CHAPTER 7

What action should I take now?

Watch the developments of Covid-19 passports over the next few months. Watch what governments are saying and for what services you will use them. Ask yourself the question, if I had to forgo that, would it cause me a problem?

Suppose we can't access a restaurant or a pub, tiny problem. If we cannot get access to supermarkets, huge problem.

At the moment, stay aware, keep in touch with me if you have any doubts. You can contact me through jamesgwhitelaw.com. We may decide to set up a forum to co-ordinate opposition if deemed necessary.

This marks the end of the book. If you have enjoyed this book, we would ask you to help us.

1. We would be grateful if you could leave a review of the book on Amazon. These reviews are the lifeblood of my business, and without them, I would have no new customers, and I could no longer write books.

2. I would welcome you to contact us through my author website at www.jamesgwhitelaw.com. I can assure you and I am a real person and do not use a pen name. I will answer any questions you have as soon as I am able.

3. Finally, let your friends know that you read my book and enjoyed it on your social media pages.

Thankyou for reading the book.